GREAT EXPECTATIONS

by
Charles Dickens

Teacher Guide

Written by
Gloria Levine, M.A.

Note

The text used to prepare this guide was the Penguin Classics softcover published by the Penguin Group, edited by Angus Calder. Introduction and notes ©1965 Penguin Books Ltd. The page references may differ in other editions.

Please note: Please assess the appropriateness of this book for the age level and maturity of your students prior to reading and discussing it with your class.

ISBN 1-56137-514-4

To order, contact your local school
supply store, or—

Novel Units, Inc.
P.O. Box 433
Bulverde, TX 78163-0433

Web site: www.educyberstor.com

Table of Contents

Novel Units: Rationale

How do you ensure that the needs of individual students are met in a heterogeneous classroom? How do you challenge students of all abilities without losing some to confusion and others to boredom?

With the push toward "untracking" our schools, there are questions that more and more educators need to examine. As any teacher of "gifted" or "remedial" students can attest, even "homogeneous" classrooms contain students with a range of abilities and interests. Here are some of the strategies research suggests:

- cooperative learning
- differentiated assignments
- questioning strategies that tap several levels of thinking
- flexible grouping within the class
- cross-curriculum integration
- process writing
- portfolio evaluation

Novel Units Teacher Guides and *Student Packets* are designed with these seven facets in mind. Discussion questions, projects, and activities are framed to span all of the levels of Bloom's Taxonomy. Graphic organizers are provided to enhance critical thinking and comprehension. Tests and quizzes (included in the Student Packets) have been developed at two levels of difficulty (Level 1=lower; Level 2=higher). While most of the activities in the Teacher Guides and Student Packets could be completed individually, many are ideal vehicles for collaborative effort.

Throughout the guides, there is an emphasis on collaboration: students helping other students to generate ideas, students working together to actualize those ideas, and students sharing their products with other students. Extension activities link literature with other areas of the curriculum—including writing, art, music, science, history, geography, and current events—and provide a basis for portfolio evaluation.

Finally, teachers are encouraged to adapt the guides to meet the needs of individual classes and students. The open-ended nature of many of the activities makes them useful for most any level.

You know your students best; we are offering you some tools for working with them. On the following page are some of the "nuts and bolts" for using these "tools": a glossary of some of the terms used above that will facilitate your use of the guides.

Bloom's Taxonomy

is a classification system for various levels of thinking. Questions keyed to these levels may be:

- comprehension questions, which ask one to state the meaning of what is written,
- application questions, which ask one to extend one's understanding to a new situation,
- analysis questions, which ask one to think about relationships between ideas such as cause/effect,
- evaluation questions, which ask one to judge the accuracy of ideas, and
- synthesis questions, which ask one to develop a product by integrating the ideas in the text with ideas of one's own.

Graphic Organizers

are visual representations of how ideas are related to each other. These "pictures"—including Venn diagrams, flow charts, attribute webs, etc.—help students collect information, make interpretations, solve problems, devise plans, and become aware of how they think.

Cooperative Learning

refers to learning activities in which groups of two or more students collaborate. There is compelling research evidence that integration of social activities into the learning process—such as small group discussion, group editing, group art projects—often leads to richer, more long-lasting learning.

Evaluation Portfolios

are, literally, portable cases for carrying loose papers and prints. More and more teachers at all levels are utilizing portfolios—product folders—in assessment of student learning.

Process Writing

is a way of teaching writing in which the emphasis is no longer on the product alone. Rather, students work continuously through the steps of prewriting, drafting, and revision—often through collaborative effort—in order to develop a piece for sharing with a real audience.

Plot Summary

The story begins in Kent, England, sometime around 1810—the time of Dickens' own childhood—and is narrated by the central character, Pip. As the story opens, the adult Pip recalls being raised after the death of his parents by his punitive sister and her husband, a gentle blacksmith named Joe.

One day a convict escaped from a nearby prison-ship and intimidated young Pip into getting him a file and some food. The convict got into a scuffle with another escaped convict and both were soon recaptured, but Pip long suffered from guilt over stealing the tool and victuals from his home. Shortly thereafter, Pumblechook—Joe's overbearing uncle, a prosperous corn chandler—arrived with an invitation for Pip from an eccentric, wealthy woman who lived in a neighboring town. Pip was taken to Miss Havisham's and was dismayed by the vision she presented. Jilted on her wedding day, she had never gone outside since—nor, apparently, had she ever taken off the wedding gown. The decaying wedding cake still sat on the table amidst the cobwebs.

This was the first of many visits Pip was to make to Miss Havisham's, where he soon fell in love with her beautiful but arrogant ward, Estella. On one visit to Miss Havisham's, Pip encountered a well-dressed boy who provoked him into a fight and Pip dispatched his opponent handily; the loser took his loss with good humor. Anxious to become a "gentleman" so that he could win Estella, Pip learned all that he could about reading and writing from Biddy, a kind orphan girl who helped Pip's sister. At 14, Pip was apprenticed to Joe and his visits to Satis—Miss Havisham's estate—ended, but his infatuation with Estella did not. After an attack by an unknown assailant (Pip suspected Orlick, a sullen employee of Joe's), Pip's sister was left a semi-invalid.

Four years later Mr. Jaggers, Miss Havisham's lawyer, informed him that an anonymous benefactor would be paying for his education to be a gentleman. Full of high hopes of fulfilling his "great expectations," Pip assumed that the benefactor was Miss Havisham, and that she intended for him to marry Estella. Pip went to London and found that his tutor's son was none other than Herbert Pocket—the boy he had fought at Miss Havisham's. Herbert told Pip the story of how Miss Havisham had sought revenge on the male sex—whose representative had so pained her 25 years ago on her wedding day—by rearing Estella to attract men and then break their hearts.

Pip and Herbert soon became best of friends and both racked up extensive debts by high living. Whenever Pip needed money, he went to Jaggers' representative, Wemmick. Wemmick, who made a hobby of collecting keepsakes from executed prisoners, invited Pip to his home, modeled after a miniature castle, and there Pip met Wemmick's beloved, senile father. On his 21st birthday, Pip was hopeful that he would learn the identity of his benefactor, but Jaggers merely handed him a check for 500 pounds and told him that he must manage his own affairs on that amount for a year.

Desirous of helping his friend Herbert, Pip secretly arranged to have Herbert set up in business with part of the money.

Meanwhile, Pip grew increasingly jealous of boorish Bentley Drummle, who seemed to be capturing Estella's favor. Pip's dreams fell apart when the convict he had helped so long ago appeared at his door one night and revealed to Pip's horror that it was he who had provided for Pip all these years. Deported to Australia, he had made a fortune as a sheep farmer. The convict also revealed that his long-ago partner, Compeyson, was hunting him down. The convict faced execution if he was discovered in England. Coincidentally, Compeyson was the same man who deserted Miss Havisham on her wedding day. Herbert helped Pip keep the convict, Magwitch *aka* "Provis," hidden, but Pip refused to take any more money from the convict.

After a scuffle with Drummle at an inn, Pip confronted Miss Havisham about leading him to believe all these years that she was his benefactor. At the same time he revealed to Estella his love for her. She told him she and Drummle were to be married soon.

Herbert and Pip made plans to row "Provis" down the river where they could put him on a steamship out of the country. Meanwhile, Jaggers invited Pip to dinner, where he received a message that Miss Havisham wanted to see him. At the same dinner, Pip suddenly realized that Molly, Jaggers' servant, was Estella's mother.

Feeling remorseful about how she had wronged both Pip and Estella, Miss Havisham agreed to Pip's request that she become Herbert's anonymous benefactor. She begged Pip to forgive her, and he did, in writing. Following an inexplicable instinct, Pip returned shortly after leaving Miss Havisham's room—and found her engulfed in flames. He smothered the fire immediately, but she was badly injured and his hands were burned.

In an exemplary Dickensian coincidence, Pip put together the pieces of the convict's verbal autobiography and realized that "Provis" was Estella's father. Molly had threatened to kill the child, and the convict had assumed she was dead. A short time later, Orlick lured Pip onto the marshes and said that he now planned to kill Pip; Herbert came to his rescue and Orlick fled.

The convict's escape was nearly realized, but at the last minute a boat appeared carrying his arch-nemesis, Compeyson. Provis and Compeyson struggled as the steamship ran into them; Compeyson drowned and Provis was badly injured. He died several days later—before his execution date, but moments before Pip told him that the daughter he thought had died in childhood had grown into the beautiful woman Pip couldn't help loving.

Pip then suffered a long illness and was nursed back to health by Joe. His friendship with Joe renewed, Pip had high hopes of marrying kind Biddy—but discovered on arriving back at his old home that Biddy and Joe had just been married.

Eleven years later, Pip visited Biddy and Joe and their children and decided to revisit Miss Havisham's deserted house one last time. There he happened to find Estella—whose brutal husband had since died. Estella was in the garden, also visiting Satis for the first time in years. After a few conciliatory words, they walked off hand in hand.

Background on the Novelist

Charles Dickens was born in Portsea, England, in 1812, the second of eight children. A precocious child, he learned to read at an early age and eagerly devoured stories by Fielding, Defoe, Goldsmith and others. His father, a clerk at the Navy Pay Office, had trouble supporting his large family. Charles was forced to work in a blacking warehouse (shoe polish factory) when he was 12—an experience that fired his determination to fight his way out of poverty.

A couple of years later, his father was arrested and imprisoned in debtors' prison for three months. Meanwhile, by age 20 Charles had become a well-respected newspaper reporter. He fell in love with a banker's daughter, but her family convinced her that he wasn't "good enough" for her and he was devastated. Under the pseudonym "Boz," Charles began writing street sketches that anticipate many of the themes later found in his novels: prisons, law courts, snobbery, sympathy for the poor.

He married his editor's daughter and shortly thereafter published his first novel, *Pickwick Papers,* a narrative in numbered installments—and became an almost overnight, world-wide success. A prolific writer, he found that his rise in social importance kept pace with his literary fame. In 1842, he and his wife traveled to the U.S., whose democracy he admired. He soon found that America was nearly as corrupt as England, and he angered many Americans by making them the targets of satire in *Martin Chuzzlewit.* By 1851, Dickens had nine children but in 1857 he began an affair with an actress (said to be cold and aloof—the model for Estella, perhaps) and his wife left him. Charles, Jr. went with his mother and the other children remained with Dickens.

He wrote *Great Expectations* in weekly installments from 1860 to 1861. Ever restless, he made extensive tours and gave readings to augment his income—despite the fact that his health had been weakened by a terrible train wreck. Further debilitated by a lucrative but exhausting American tour, he suffered a stroke at dinner in 1870 and died the next morning at age 58.

Initiating Activities

Choose one or more of the following activities to establish an appropriate mind set for the story students are about to read:

1. **Anticipation Guide** (See *Novel Units Student Packet,* Activity #1): Students rate and discuss their opinions of statements which tap themes they will meet in the story.

   1———— 2 ———— 3 ———— 4 ———— 5 ———— 6

   agree strongly   disagree strongly

   Sample statements:
   _____a. Love is blind.
   _____b. Unbalanced parents have unbalanced children.
   _____c. It takes money to live the good life.
   _____d. The lives of the well-to-do are empty.

2. **Video:** Watch the 1946 black and white version (directed by David Lean, with John Mills as Pip, Jean Simmons as young Estella, and Alec Guiness as Herbert Pocket), or the 1988 BBC version directed by Julian Aymes. The latter is five hours long—but includes every plot convolution (and there are many!)

3. **Log:** Have students keep a response log as they read.
   a) In one type of log, the student assumes the persona of one of the characters. Writing on one side of each piece of paper, the student writes in the first person ("I...") about his/her reactions to one episode in that chapter. A partner (or the teacher) responds to these writings on the other side of the paper, as if talking to the student.
   b) In the dual entry log, students jot down brief summaries and reactions to each section of the novel they have read. (The first entry could be made based on a preview of the novel—a glance at the cover and a flip through the book.)

Pages	Summary	Reactions
		These might begin: "I liked the part where...", "This reminded me of the time I...", "This character reminds me of ...," etc.

4. **Verbal Scales:** After students finish a section of the story, have them chart their feelings/judgments about various characters using the following scales or others you construct. Students should discuss their ratings, using evidence from the story.

Like	1 2 3 4 5 6	Dislike
Happy	1 2 3 4 5 6	Sad
Active	1 2 3 4 5 6	Passive
Honest	1 2 3 4 5 6	Dishonest
Caring	1 2 3 4 5 6	Unkind
Responsible	1 2 3 4 5 6	Irresponsible
Proud	1 2 3 4 5 6	Humble
Rich	1 2 3 4 5 6	Poor
Sympathetic	1 2 3 4 5 6	Self-absorbed

5. **Brainstorming:** Have students generate associations with the word "infatuation," a theme that is central to the story, while a student scribe jots ideas around the central word on a large piece of paper or on the chalkboard. Help students "cluster" the ideas into categories. A sample framework is shown below.

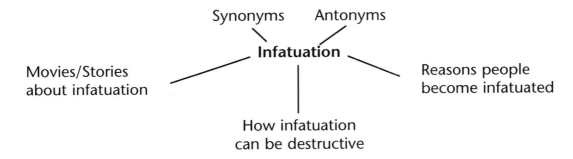

6. **Role Play:** Have small groups of students improvise skits demonstrating one of the following situations (analogous to a situation that is central to the story):

- An adult intimidates a child by telling him what "the bogey man" will do to him if he doesn't obey.
- A pretty, arrogant young woman mistreats a young man whom she knows has a crush on her.
- An old woman who was jilted long ago warns a young woman against men.

7. **Geography:** Have students examine or create a map showing the general setting of the story. Have them locate specific towns depicted in the story (Rochester, Cooling, London, etc.).

8. **Discussion:**
   - **Of Dickens' time:** This is a long book (over 500 pages, with notes). How was Dickens' time different from ours? What distractions do we have—e.g. TV, radio—that readers did not have in those days? What are some of the advantages that a long novel has over a shorter one? What can the author do that he doesn't have enough room for in a shorter version?

   - **Of Poverty and Wealth:** How would you define "poverty"? Are those who have money generally happier than those who do not? What problems do the poor have that others do not? What do you think is the worst thing about being poor? Are poor children less likely to be spoiled than rich ones? Are poor children any more likely to be kind and sensible or unkind and violent than rich ones? How was poverty different in Dickensian England than it is in the U.S. today? Would you keep working if you ended up with a lot of money, say from an inheritance or lottery winnings? Would you help poor people with any of your wealth?

   - **Of Lawyers, Courts, Prisons:** What were law courts like in Dickens' day? How were prisoners treated? What sorts of punishments were meted out? What were the prisons like? What are they like today?

9. **Prereading Research:** Selected students (perhaps those in need of extra-credit points) should do some research on the following topics and report back to the whole group:
   a) schools in Dickens's day (for comparison with Pip's schooling)
   b) The Affecting Tragedy of George Barnwell—a play by George Lillo (in which Wopsle acts)
   c) Newgate Prison (to which many of Jaggers' clients are sent)

10. **Prediction:** Have students predict what the story might be about based on the title and cover illustration. What will the mood of the story probably be? Based on the cover painting, when does the story take place? What does it mean to have "great expectations"? Do you think the "great expectations" in the story will be realized?

11. **Writing:** What "great expectations" do you have for your future? Imagine you are now 38 years old. Your 20th high school reunion is coming up. You're unable to attend, so you write a short autobiographical sketch telling fellow students what's happened to you since you graduated.

Vocabulary, Discussion Questions, Writing Ideas, Activities

Chapters 1-7 pages 35-83

Vocabulary
(Please see pages 30-32 for an extensive vocabulary list. The words listed for each section correlate to vocabulary activities in the Student Packet, but there are many words in this novel with which students will not be familiar.)

trenchant 42	remonstrance 43	augmented 45	emphatic 46
reproachful 46	imprecations 52	dissuading 54	contumaciously 59
imperiously 60	execrating 67	pilfering 71	exonerated 71
venerated 74	erudition 7	perspicuity 77	sagaciously 78
ablutions 83			

Vocabulary Activity
Word mapping is an activity that lends itself to any vocabulary list. For words that have clear antonyms, the following framework is suitable:

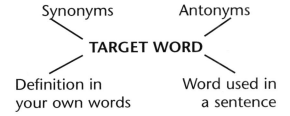

Variation: Instead of listing antonyms, students can provide line drawings, symbols, or magazine cut-outs to illustrate the target word.

Discussion Questions
1. Who is the narrator and what is your impression of him? *The narrator is Philip—Pip, an orphan now grown; the well-spoken narrator describes his boyhood fears with a wry, self-deprecating sense of humor.*

2. With what frightening childhood memory does the narrator begin his tale? *While examining his parents' and brothers' graves, Pip is accosted by a fearsome escaped convict who commands him to procure food and a file.*

3. What is Pip's home life like? How is he treated? *Pip lives with his harsh older sister and her gentle blacksmith husband, Joe Gargery; Pip's sister constantly criticizes and punishes Pip while Joe loves and tries to protect the boy.*

4. Why does Joe think that Pip has been "bolting his food"? Why does that bother Joe? *Joe notices that Pip's bread—which he is secretly saving for the convict—has disappeared; Joe is worried that eating so fast might injure Pip's health.*

---

5. What sort of "elixir" does Mrs. Joe give Pip? Why? *She gives him Tar-water to counteract the effects of bolting his food.* Does Mrs. Joe's faith in elixirs remind you of any other characters you have met in literature? *perhaps Tom Sawyer's Aunt Polly*

6. What does Pip steal from his sister's house? Why? *He steals a file, some bread, cheese, mincemeat, brandy, a pork pie; the convict has threatened to send someone after him if he doesn't bring food and a file.* Would you have done the same thing, in his place? What do you think would have happened if he had been caught?

7. Pip meets someone on the marsh and thinks "It's the young man." (p. 49) What young man? Why does Pip "dare say I should have felt a pain in my liver, too, if I had known where it was." In what tone of voice do you imagine the adult Pip saying this? *The adult Pip mocks himself gently for his childish fear of the young man the convict threatened to send after Pip to pluck out his heart and liver.*

8. How does the convict act when Pip brings the food? Are you surprised by his reaction? Is Pip surprised? Do you feel any sympathy for the convict at this point? Does Pip? *He gobbles the food and tears come to his eyes; Pip is frightened still but pities the convict.*

9. What is the Christmas celebration at Pip's house like? Does he enjoy it? Would you? *Pip's aunt makes a special dinner and invites guests; Pip is too worried about the discovery of the stolen food to enjoy dinner; besides, the adults continually criticize and correct him.*

10. Why do the soldiers come to the door? What do you think would have happened to Pip if the soldiers hadn't shown up at that moment? *The soldiers need Joe to apply his blacksmithing skills to a broken pair of handcuffs they plan to use on the convicts when they are captured.*

11. After the soldiers arrive, how can you tell that both Pip and Joe feel pity for the convicts? Why do you think that is? *As the search gets underway, both say they hope the convicts aren't found.* If there were an escaped convict around your house, wouldn't you want him or her captured?

12. What are the two convicts doing when they are discovered? How do they seem to feel about each other? *"Pip's convict" is struggling with the other one, who claims "he tried to murder me."* Why do you suppose that is?

13. What lie does the convict tell before he is put on the prison boat? How do you know it is a lie? Why do you think he tells it? What does that show you about him? *Apparently wanting to shield Pip from getting into trouble, the convict announces that he stole food from the blacksmith's.*

14. Pip experiences internal conflict after stealing the food and file. How is he "torn"? Why doesn't he tell Joe the truth? Based on what you know of Joe so far, how do you think he would respond to Pip's admission of the truth? *He wants to tell Joe about stealing the items, but is afraid that Joe will never trust him again if he does.*

15. What is Pip's schooling like? Do you think he enjoys it? From whom does he learn the most? *He attends an evening school taught by a confused, sleepy old woman; it is her orphaned granddaughter, Biddy, who teaches Pip most of what he learns about reading, writing, and spelling.*

16. How does Joe feel about his wife? Why do you think he puts up with the way she treats him? *Joe speaks admiringly of his wife and doesn't complain of her abuse; Joe remembers how his father abused his mother, and Joe doesn't ever want to risk doing wrong by his own wife.* Would you consider him an "abused husband"? What advice would you give him, if he were a friend of yours in today's world?

17. Who is Miss Havisham and why does she want to see Pip? Why is Pip's sister so anxious that he should go? How does Pip feel about going? *Miss Havisham is an eccentric, reclusive, wealthy old woman who has decided she wants to see a boy play; Pip's sister hopes the visit will make Pip's fortune; Pip is puzzled and confused.*

PREDICTION: What will Miss Havisham be like? How will Pip "play" at Miss Havisham's?

Writing Activity: Interior Monologue
Write what you sense to be Pip's thoughts and feelings as he sits at the Christmas table, anticipating that his sister will discover the theft at any moment.

Critical Thinking: Character Attribute Webs
Attribute webs are simply a visual representation of a character's traits. They provide a systematic way for students to organize and recap the information they have about that particular character. Attribute webs may be used after reading the story or completed gradually as information unfolds—done individually, or finished as a group project—as the basis for discussion, or as a pre-writing activity.

Writers tell readers about their characters by showing—
* what the characters themselves do,
* what the characters themselves say,
* how other characters react to them, and
* how they look and act through direct description in expository passages.

Using one type of attribute web, students organize thoughts and details around these four categories. In another type, students use separate webs for separate categories of traits, such as traits revealed by character's actions, traits revealed by character's appearance, and traits revealed by what others say about the character. Advanced students can add extensions for citation of specific details and examples.

Examples of both types of webs appear below.

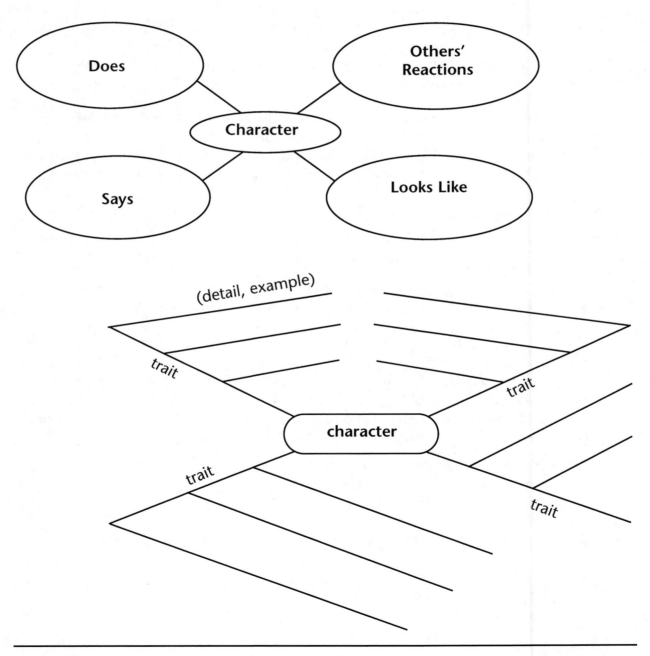

Chapters 8-12   pages 83-126

Vocabulary

gourmandising 84   transfixed 91   capricious 92   ignominiously 95
adamantine 95   felicitous 101   appalled 120   sanguinary 121
trepidation 121   unremunerative 125

Discussion Questions

1. What kind of host is Mr. Pumblechook? Why is Pip glad when it is time to leave for Miss Havisham's? *Pumblechook gives Pip an uncomfortable bed and a meager breakfast, and enjoys intimidating him with math problems, warnings, and criticisms.*

2. What do Pip and Estella seem to think of each other? Why do you suppose Miss Havisham doesn't tell Estella to be more polite to their guest? *Pip finds Estella pretty and snobbish; she arrogantly calls him a "common labouring-boy." Miss Havisham enjoys Estella's nastiness.*

3. What is strange about Miss Havisham and her surroundings? Why do you suppose Pip doesn't just run away from this strange scene? *Miss Havisham is in a yellowed wedding dress, the wedding cake is decaying on the table, and the clocks are all stopped at twenty minutes to nine.*

4. Miss Havisham says that she wants "diversion." Does Pip succeed in providing that for her? How or why not? *Uncomfortable, Pip tells her that he cannot play, but agrees to a game of cards with Estella.*

5. How does Pip feel after his visit with Miss Havisham? Why do you suppose he doesn't have a "thicker skin"? Why doesn't he let Estella's insults "roll off his back"? *He feels depressed, humiliated, ashamed of his clothes, manners, and background.*

6. How and why does Pip exaggerate in telling about his trip to Miss Havisham's? *Pip feels that it would be coarse to reveal what he really has seen, so he makes up an elaborate story about a black velvet coach and four dogs.*

7. Why does Pip admit to Joe—but not to his sister and Pumblechook—that his stories about Miss Havisham's are lies? *Pip trusts Joe and cares what Joe thinks of him, so Pip wants to be honest with Joe.*

8. What "special agreement" does Pip make with Joe regarding Joe's education? *They will keep quiet about any learning Joe does, since Joe's wife might fear that he would "rise."*

9. How does Pip know that the stranger in the Jolly Bargeman knows "Pip's convict"? What does the stranger give Pip? *The stranger stirs his drink with the file Pip had given the convict and gives Pip a shilling wrapped in two one-pound notes.* Are you surprised that Joe and his wife intend to return the notes to the stranger?

10. What does Pip mean by describing the three ladies and one gentleman at Miss Havisham's as "toadies and humbugs"? *All are bowing and scraping to keep in Miss Havisham's good graces in hopes of getting an inheritance when she dies.* (p. 109) Who are Camilla and Raymond criticizing? What are their complaints against him? *They are critical of Matthew Pocket, who apparently didn't buy mourning trimmings for his children when a relative died.*

11. What work does Miss Havisham have Pip do? Does he mind? *She tells him to walk her around the room. He doesn't complain, but doesn't like parading in front of the relatives.*

12. How does Miss Havisham seem to feel about her visitors? *She grows impatient with them and sees through their false declarations of affection.*

13. Why do Pip and the "pale young gentleman" fight? What is the outcome? Why isn't Pip happier about being the victor? *The pale young gentleman invites Pip to fight and butts him in the stomach. His victory leaves Pip feeling like an uncivilized savage.*

14. Why do you think Estella tells Pip he may kiss her? Why doesn't Pip enjoy the kiss? *She enjoyed watching him fight the stranger; Pip feels that the kiss is offered mechanically.* Do you think Pip is wrong to accept a "worthless" kiss?

15. Why does Miss Havisham want to see Joe? *She notices how tall Pip is growing and wants to talk with Joe about having Pip apprenticed at once.*

PREDICTION: The adult narrator says that he "could have had no foresight then, that [the burly man he met at Miss Havisham's] ever would be anything to me." (p. 111) How do you think their paths cross in the future? The adult narrator also says that he now knows "the pain [Estella] cost me afterwards." How do you think she hurts him later?

Writing Activity: Suppose that Miss Havisham were telling the story. Describe Pip's second visit to Satis—from Miss Havisham's point of view.

Vocabulary

diabolical 131	affront 140	maudlin 145	benefactor 145
surmising 146	corroborated 148	aberration 150	propitiation 151
pugilistic 168	placable 169		

Discussion Questions

1. What do Joe and Miss Havisham talk about? What does she give Pip? How much is that in American money? *Miss Havisham asks Joe if Pip likes the blacksmithing trade, and gives Pip 25 guineas as the "premium" he has earned by coming to her; today, a guinea=about $3; 25 guineas=about $75.*

2. Why does Pumblechook take Pip to the Town Hall? Why does Pip feel like a criminal? *Pumblechook trundles him off—pushing him as if he were a criminal—to be "bound"—to file in court the legal papers for his indenture.*

3. How has Pip's attitude toward his home and toward blacksmithing changed? Why? *Pip is now ashamed of his home and no longer likes blacksmithing; he wants to be "worthy" of Estella.*

4. Why doesn't Joe think it is a good idea for Pip to continue to visit Miss Havisham? *She has said that she will give him no more money and Joe doesn't want it to look as if Pip expects more.*

5. Who is Orlick? How can you tell that he doesn't like Pip or Pip's sister? Why does he dislike them? *Orlick is a sinister man who works for Joe; he throws sparks Pip's way and calls Pip's sister a "foul shrew;" Orlick probably thinks that newly apprenticed Pip will someday replace him and Orlick hates Pip's sister for calling him an "idle hulker" when Joe gives Orlick a half-holiday.*

6. What happens to Pip's sister? Why does Pip, with his head "full of George Barnwell," believe that he is a suspect in the crime? Why does he worry that he unwittingly provided the instrument for the attack? *Pip's sister is hit over the head; Mr. Wopsle has been reading him the story of an apprentice who murders his uncle and Pumblechook has been telling Pip to "take warning" from the story; a convict's leg iron had been used as the weapon and Pip believes that it is the same one he enabled the convict to remove some time ago.*

7. How does Pip's sister change after the attack? How does the household change? *She becomes quieter and gentler; her hearing, speech, and memory are impaired; Biddy arrives and organizes the household.*

8. What is Biddy like? What does she think of Pip's plans to become a "gentleman"? *Biddy is sensible and good; she asks him if he might not be happier just as he is.*

9. Why doesn't Biddy like Orlick? *He "dances" at her, trying to get her attention.* Why doesn't Pip try to have Orlick dismissed? *For some reason, Pip's sister suddenly seems quite attached to Orlick.*

10. Why does the "strange gentleman" request a private conference with Pip and Joe? *The lawyer wants to tell Pip and Joe that Pip has an anonymous benefactor.*

11. Where has Pip heard the name of his tutor before? *During his visits to Miss Havisham, he has heard the Pockets criticizing "Matthew"—the man Jaggers mentions as a suitable tutor.*

12. Why does Pip assume that Miss Havisham is his secret benefactor? What reasons do you suppose she might have for wanting to remain anonymous? How does Pip feel about leaving home? *He has hinted to her that he would like to become a gentleman; she is the only wealthy person he knows; he is excited, and somewhat anxious, about leaving home.*

PREDICTION: Pip speculates about what "might have been" between Biddy and him if he hadn't met Estella. Do you think he will ever get together with Biddy? What will happen to Pip's sister? How will Pip's training as a gentleman go?

Writing Activity: Imagine that Biddy keeps a journal. Write the entry she makes the night before Pip leaves for London.

Chapters 19-23   pages 173-219

Vocabulary

obscurely 173	audacious 177	affable 181	unwonted 182
guileless 194	dolefully 198	avaricious 202	genteel 203
compress 204	unreservedly 205	incipient 209	amiable 210
abashed 217	irrepressible 217	odious 219	

Discussion Questions

1. What preparations does Pip make for his journey? How does Mr. Trabb's attitude toward Pip change? How does Mr. Pumblechook's attitude change? Why? *Pip takes the money Jaggers has given him to get outfitted for the trip; Trabb becomes obsequious when he learns of Pip's money; Pumblechook, too, tries to ingratiate himself and suggests that he could use a "sleeping partner."*

2. Why doesn't Joe walk with Pip to the coach? *Pip tells Joe he wishes to walk alone; Pip is embarrassed to be seen with Joe.*

3. What is Mr. Jaggers' office in London like? When you read the description (p. 188), how does it make you feel? *The office is gloomy and littered with morbid mementoes such as a rusty pistol and some death heads.*

4. How does Mr. Jaggers treat his clients? How do they act toward him? *He treats them arrogantly, while they grovel.*

5. What are your impressions of Mr. Wemmick? Do you like him? Does Pip? *At this point, he seems stiff and officious; he has a morbid hobby of collecting "portable property" such as mourning rings from prisoners who have been executed; Pip isn't very comfortable with Mr. Wemmick yet.*

6. What is the contrast between what the Barnard inn turns out to be like—and what Pip had hoped his new living situation would be? *It is much dingier and more run down than he had imagined it would be.*

7. Why is Mr. Pocket, Junior, out when Pip arrives? Why are Pip and Mr. Pocket, Junior, surprised when they see each other? *Herbert is out buying fruit for Pip; they recognize each other from the fight they had at Miss Havisham's.*

8. What does Herbert reveal to Pip about Miss Havisham's past? Why have Herbert's father and Miss Havisham been at odds? *She had been engaged 25 years ago, but her fiancé sent her a letter on their wedding day calling off the wedding. Herbert's father, Matthew, was the only relative to warn her that she was doing too much for her fiancé—and she angrily ordered Matthew out of the house, as a result.*

9. What does Pip ask Herbert to teach him at dinner? *more genteel table manners*

10. What does Herbert choose to call Pip and why? What does this show you about Herbert? *Handel; good-natured, well-read Herbert doesn't like the name Philip because it reminds him of a character in a moralistic story for children; for this former blacksmith, he prefers the name of the composer who wrote "The Harmonious Blacksmith."*

11. Besides Pip, who else rooms in Herbert's house? *Bentley Drummle, a sullen, heavyset heir of a baronet, and Startop, a younger man*

12. What is Herbert's family like? Would you like to be a member of that family? *It is a chaotic household with children scrambling everywhere; the mother fails to pay much attention to the children and prefers to talk about the nobility and what might have been had she married someone of higher station; the father is kind but overwhelmed.*

PREDICTION: How will Pip get along with Herbert? with his tutor, Herbert's father? with Drummle and Startop, the other two boarders?

Writing Activity: Follow Pip to his room after he leaves Matthew Pocket at the end of the chapter. Describe what the room is like, what Pip takes out of his portmanteau, and what his thoughts are as he prepares for bed.

Chapters 24-30   pages 219-273

Vocabulary

| niggardly 225 | adversary 238 | spurious 247 | rankled 258 |
| reticence 263 | abased 264 | despondency 269 | |

Discussion Questions

1. Does Pip have a high opinion of his tutor? What do you think makes a good teacher? *Pip admires and trusts Matthew, who is honest, enthusiastic, and encouraging.*

2. What are the "horrible heads" in Mr. Jaggers' office? Why do you suppose he keeps them? *They are masks made from casts of the heads of executed criminals.*

3. Why is Pip curious about dining with Mr. Jaggers? *Mr. Wemmick has told him to pay special attention to the housekeeper.*

4. Why does Pip like Startop more than Drummle? What is the contrast between the two young men? *Drummle is sulky, proud, and suspicious and comes from a wealthy family; Startop is delicate, devoted to the mother who spoiled him.*

5. Why do the Pockets—except for Herbert's family—hate Pip? *They believe that Miss Havisham is spending money on Pip that she should have given to them, her family members.*

6. What is Wemmick's home like? What does it "say" about him? Are you surprised that he has this sort of home? *It shows that he is more soft-hearted and imaginative than he seems; he has rigged it up into the model of a tiny castle—in part to delight his old father.*

7. Why does Jaggers' housekeeper remind Pip of something from *Macbeth*? How does she act? *With her streaming hair and disturbed expression, she reminds Pip of the witches in Macbeth.*

8. How does Jaggers show his interest in Drummle? Why do you think Jaggers is so interested in Drummle? *He asks Pip about Drummle, says he likes the look of him; perhaps he recognizes that Drummle's ruthlessness will make him a "winner" in certain circles.*

9. Why does Drummle almost come to blows with Startop at Jaggers' house? Why do you think Jaggers says that he likes Drummle, nevertheless? *Pip remarks that Drummle borrowed money from Startop and when Startop agreeably tries to change the subject, Drummle starts to throw a glass at Startop. Perhaps Jaggers admires Drummle's brutality and egotism, and sees it as strength.*

10. Why does Biddy write to Pip? *to let him know that Joe is coming to visit*

11. Why does Joe come to visit Pip? Why doesn't Joe stay longer? How do you think Pip feels after Joe leaves? *Miss Havisham sends the message that Estella is home and that Pip may visit her; Joe feels uncomfortable in London and senses that he makes Pip uncomfortable; Pip feels momentarily guilty.*

12. Who sits in the coach with Pip? Why is Pip so frightened? *two convicts—one of whom is the convict who gave him the money at the inn, after making it clear that he knew the convict Pip had helped*

13. Who is Miss Havisham's porter? How does Pip have him fired—and why? *Orlick; Pip, who distrusts Jaggers, tells Jaggers—Miss Havisham's lawyer—that Orlick is unfit for the post.*

14. Does Estella encourage Pip? Do you think she is "leading him on"? Why is he so infatuated with her, still? Why does Miss Havisham tell Pip to love Estella? Does she think they are "meant for each other"? *Estella tolerates him and "lures him on," but still treats him like a boy. Miss Havisham wants Estella to break Pip's heart, as hers was broken years ago.*

15. What is Herbert's advice about Estella? Do you think that his is good advice? What is his own love life like? *He asks Pip if Pip couldn't try to detach himself. He is in love with Clara, and secretly engaged to marry her.*

PREDICTION: When—if ever—will Estella begin to be interested in Pip? Will they get together?

Writing Activity: Dickens includes several minor characters in this story—such as Sarah Pocket and Trabb's boy. Imagine that the life of one of these characters had been developed by Dickens. Describe what that life has been like and why the character is as he or she is now.

Vocabulary

elocution 276	approbation 277	fetters 280	cistern 281
subordinate 283	turnkeys 283	suppliants 284	pattens 285
ostler 288	farthingale 290	interment 297	quarries 302
pilgrimage 311	Union Jack 311	cestus 316	

Discussion Questions

1. What play does Pip go to see? Why? How does he like it? *Hamlet; Mr. Wopsle is in it; he tries to applaud, but finds the show as ludicrous as everyone else does.*

2. Why does Estella write to Pip? Does he mind being asked that favor? Should he? *She directs him to meet her carriage in London and accompany her to Richmond. He is delighted.*

3. What is Newgate? How does Pip react to what he sees? *prison; He is horrified and disgusted.*

4. Why is Estella going to Richmond? *There she is to live with a rich woman who will introduce her to society.*

5. Do you think Estella feels bitter toward Miss Havisham for the way she brought Estella up? Should she? *She grows angry as she describes Miss Havisham as an "impostor of a woman"—p. 287.*

6. What are some of the negative influences that Pip's "expectations" have on him and on Herbert? How do they get into debt? *Pip spends money without learning an honest way to earn it; he and Herbert buy expensive furniture, join a club, buy expensive meals, etc.*

7. Is Pip sorry when his sister dies? Where will Biddy go now? *He is relieved; Biddy will try to get a teaching job.*

8. Why does Pip get angry with Biddy after the funeral? With whom do you side? *She contradicts him when he says that he will visit Joe more often.*

9. How does Pip's relationship with Jaggers change when Pip "comes of age"? *Jaggers gives him some money and tells him that he must live off of that for a year— on his own, now.*

10. Who is Miss Skiffins? Do you think she and Wemmick are well-suited? *Wemmick's lady friend, she too is orderly and polite. They seem a matched pair.*

---

11. What advice does Pip seek from Wemmick? Why does Pip want to help Herbert? How does Wemmick help Pip accomplish that? *Pip wants to know how he might help Herbert financially; Wemmick contacts Miss Skiffins's brother, an accountant.*

PREDICTION: Pip feels a "nameless shadow" pass when he sees Estella's face at the window of the coach. What do you think that fleeting thought or memory might be?

Writing Activity: Pip has an anxiety-ridden dream the night after he goes to see Mr. Wopsle's play (p. 279). Describe the images and conversations that take place in the dream. Then describe a frightening dream you have had.

Chapters 38-43   pages 318-372

Vocabulary
wan 321	sconces 321	ingrate 322	beseeching 324
untenable 326	dram 343	prolix 344	dubiously 345
uncouth 346	physiognomy 349	expatriated 351	pannikins 352
pretext 358	transport 359	vagrancy 362	extenuated 367
insolent 370	superciliously 371		

Discussion Questions
1. Why do Estella and Miss Havisham argue (pp. 322-323)? Do you think Miss Havisham is to blame for the way she raised Estella—or was she doing the best she could? *Miss Havisham wants Estella to show her more affection and Estella accuses Miss Havisham of raising her to be cold.*

2. Why is Pip jealous of Bentley Drummle? Why do you think Estella encourages Drummle? *Drummle has been seeing Estella. Perhaps she is just trying to make Pip jealous—but Drummle's wealth is attractive also.*

3. Why does the convict come to see Pip? How does Pip treat his guest? What does he learn about how the convict made his fortune? *The convict reveals that he is Pip's benefactor. Pip, repelled by his guest, plans at first to put him out; when he learns about how the convict lived at various trades around the world—saving his money to send to Pip—Pip guiltily resigns himself to protecting the man.*

4. Why is Pip so upset to realize who his real benefactor is? *He had hoped that Miss Havisham had been preparing him to marry Estella and now his dreams are dashed.*

5. What danger is the convict in? Does Pip feel a responsibility to protect the convict? Do you think Pip is doing the right thing in hiding the convict? *The convict has been sentenced to death should he return to England; yes, Pip feels responsible.*

6. Why does Pip feel that he can't accept any more money from the convict? Would you take the money? *Pip feels that it is wrong to accept money that may have been made illegally.*

7. Why does the convict hate Compeyson so much? *The suave Compeyson was once his criminal partner, but blackmailed him and was let off with much more lenience by the judge than was the convict—even though Compeyson was the mastermind.*

8. How is Compeyson connected with Miss Havisham? *Compeyson is the one who jilted her, after luring her brother Arthur into a scheme to get money from her.*

9. After the convict arrives, why does Pip plan a trip to see Estella? *He wants to see her once more before leaving the country with the convict.*

10. Why are Drummle and Pip traveling in the same direction? *Both are going to see Estella.*

PREDICTION: What do you think Drummle means by snidely asking Pip if he hasn't lost enough already? (p. 371) What do you think will happen to the convict?

Writing Activity: Write a letter of advice to Pip telling him what you think he ought to do about the convict—and about Estella.

Chapters 44-50   pages 372-419

Vocabulary

plaited 380	superannuated 387	truculent 389	necromantic 397
tremulous 408	blighted 409	absolve 410	entreated 410
commiseration 412	presentiment 413	vestige 415	

Discussion Questions:

1. Pip confronts Miss Havisham about letting him believe that she was his benefactor. Has she led him on? Does he have a right to be angry? Does she seem sorry? *She admits that she let him believe the lie, but cries out angrily, "Who am I to be kind?"*

2. How does Estella explain why she plans to marry Drummle and not Pip? How does he take it? What does Miss Havisham seem to think of the wedding plans? *She knows that Drummle won't even feel her incapacity to love him—while Pip would be hurt by it; he cries bitterly; Miss Havisham looks on with pity and remorse.*

3. What favor does Pip ask of Miss Havisham? Are you surprised that she doesn't refuse? *He asks her to be Herbert's anonymous benefactor.*

4. What is in the note Wemmick sends Pip? Why does he send it? Do you think he is to be trusted? Does Pip? *Wemmick has written Pip to tell him not to go home as Wemmick has learned that Pip's rooms are being watched—and that the convict's enemy, Compeyson, is in London.*

5. What plan does Herbert come up with for hiding the convict? Why does Wemmick refer to the convict as "Tom, Jack, or Richard" while explaining the plan to Pip? *He takes the convict to the house where Clara cares for her father; there is a room to let overlooking the river; Wemmick doesn't want to admit out loud that he knows the name of the convict.*

6. Why does Herbert consider it a "blessing...for the son of my father and mother, to love a girl who has no relations..." (p. 389)? *His own family life is so chaotic.*

7. How does the convict feel about going abroad? Is he afraid to die? *He doesn't want to die, but trusts Pip and is resolved to go abroad.*

8. What plan does Pip have for getting the convict out of the country? How does he prepare? *They will row regularly past the convict's window so that he can give a window-shade signal that all is well; when the ship comes, they will quickly row the convict out to it without arousing suspicion.*

9. What distressing news does Pip get from Mr. Wopsle after watching Wopsle's play? *Compeyson was at the play, right behind Pip.*

10. When and how does Pip realize that Jaggers' housekeeper is Estella's mother? What does he learn from Wemmick about the woman and her child? *He puts two and two together after noticing the resemblance between the two women's faces and hands a couple of times; Wemmick explains that the woman had been accused of killing another woman in a jealous rage—and disposing of her child to spite her husband.*

11. Why do you think Miss Havisham gives Pip the money for Herbert? Has Miss Havisham changed since she first met Pip? *She is penitent for having caused him so much pain; she realizes now that she has wronged both Pip and Estella.*

12. What does Miss Havisham have Pip sign? Do you think he really forgives her? What does this show you about him? *His feelings are genuine as he signs the paper saying that he forgives her.*

13. How is Miss Havisham injured? What would have happened if Pip hadn't returned when he did to her room? Why did he return? *After a feeling of foreboding, Pip returns to reassure himself that she is all right; she probably would have died if he hadn't discovered that her dress had caught fire.*

14. In talking with Provis/Magwitch, what does Herbert learn about the convict's wife? How does Pip figure out that Provis is Estella's father? Do you find this coincidence too far-fetched to be believable—or does it enhance the story? *Herbert learns that the convict's wife was tried for murdering another woman after swearing to destroy her own child. Jaggers was her lawyer; Pip realizes that the story matches what Wemmick told him about Jaggers' housekeeper.*

PREDICTION: Will Pip tell Estella—or the convict—what he knows about their relationship?

Writing Activity: Pip is devastated by the news that Estella plans to get married. Write the love poem he might write after he learns of her plans.

Chapters 51-56   pages 420-470

Vocabulary

obdurate 423	retrospectively 424	limekiln 432	malignity 435
gainsaying 442	tithe 445	hawsers 446	vacillating 452
adjured 454	querulous 458	portentous 460	exordium 460
discreet 463	bagatelle 464	scourge 467	proscribed 467
appeals 468	malefactors 468	reconnoitre 453	festooned 447

Discussion Questions

1. How does Jaggers explain his role in giving Estella to Miss Havisham? Do you think he did the right thing? Do you think that Estella's father and mother should be told that they are dwelling near each other in London and that their daughter is alive and well? *Jaggers explains that he knew that Miss Havisham wanted a child— and he had seen the terrible lives led by the children of many criminals.*

2. Of what has Pumblechook managed to convince the landlord—and most of the others in the town where Pip was raised—about his role in Pip's fortune? *Pumblechook has let it be known that Pip's good fortune is due to him—and that Pip is an ingrate.*

3. Who is the dirty letter (p. 430) from? Do you think that Pip is foolish to go to the sluice-house alone? *Orlick*

4. Why does Orlick hate Pip so much? According to Orlick, why was the attack on Pip's sister Pip's "doing"? Why does Herbert show up? What would have happened if he hadn't arrived when he did? *Orlick knows that Pip got him fired from Miss Havisham's—and he feels that Pip has also come between Biddy and himself. Herbert found the note and thought it odd; Orlick would have killed Pip and burned him in the kiln.*

5. What is Pip and Herbert's plan for getting the convict to the boat? Why doesn't it work? *They plan to row him out to any foreign steamer that comes their way and will take them up; Compeyson has alerted the authorities, who try to arrest the convict before he gets on the steamer.*

6. How does Compeyson die? How is the convict injured? *The convict knocks Compeyson into the water, both struggle, and Compeyson drowns; the convict is cut on the head and chest by the keel of the steamer.*

7. Why does Herbert have to leave Pip? What do you think Herbert would say and do if he knew where the money to advance his career had come from? *Herbert's work is taking him to Cairo.*

8. Why does Wemmick decide to take his first holiday in twelve years? *He is getting married.*

9. As the convict lies dying, what does Pip tell him? How has Pip changed in his feelings toward the convict? *Pip feels affection and gratitude, not repugnance; Pip tells him that his daughter is alive and is a beautiful lady whom Pip loves.*

PREDICTION: What will happen to Pip now? Will he see Estella again?

Writing Activity: Write a news report describing the exciting capture of Magwitch, *aka* Provis, wanted criminal. Provide background information on why he was wanted by the law. Include some comments about Magwitch and Compeyson by acquaintances who were interviewed for the report.

Chapters 57-59 and Appendices   pages 470-498

Vocabulary

interminable 471	transformations 472	orthographical 474	remonstrance 474
codicil 474	evasively 477	slacken 479	perplexity 479
vestige 480	assiduity 482	ostentatious 483	debilitating 484
beguiled 486	irrevocable 487		

Discussion Questions

1. Why does Joe come to Pip after the convict dies? What sort of illness does Pip seem to have? *Joe comes to nurse Pip when he falls ill with fever and delirium.*

2. What has happened to Miss Havisham? Do you think Pip grieves for her? *She has died during Pip's illness.*

3. Why did Miss Havisham leave money to Matthew? How does that make Pip feel? How has Miss Havisham provided for the other Pockets, in her will? *Pip is happy about "the only good thing" he has done; Miss Havisham left money to Matthew after hearing Pip's account of his tutor; she left small amounts of money to the other Pockets—with pointed directions for their use, e.g. "to Miss Sarah, 25 pounds a year for pills on account of being bilious"—p. 475.*

4. What has happened to Orlick? *He is in jail after breaking into Pumblechook's house.*

5. Does Joe know who Pip's patron was? Does he know why the convict left money to Pip? How does he feel about what he knows? *Joe won't admit all that he knows, but he knows the main outline of the story; he doesn't choose to go into details, just wants Pip to know that he doesn't judge him.*

6. Why does Joe grow more uncomfortable as Pip grows stronger? *Perhaps Joe worries that as Pip gets better, he will grow cold and cast him off.*

7. Why does Joe leave without saying good-bye? Why does Pip decide to return home three days later? What surprise does he have when he gets there? *Joe figures that Pip is well now and he doesn't want to intrude; Pip decides to see if Biddy will marry him.*

8. Do you think Pip is really happy for Joe and Biddy? Do you think he is jealous? How do you think Joe would have reacted if Pip had earlier mentioned his own hopes for marrying Biddy? *Pip seems genuinely happy for Joe and Biddy.*

9. How does Pip spend the next 11 years? Do you think he is happy? Why do you suppose he never marries during that time? *Pip sells all he has and leaves England to join Herbert; he works hard and is tolerably content.*

10. What has Pip heard about Estella's marriage? *He has heard that her husband used her with great cruelty, and was killed in an accident after mistreating a horse.*

11. How does Pip happen to see Estella again? How has her attitude changed? *Pip returns to Satis and finds Estella outside; her touch is now friendly; she realizes what she "threw away" by snubbing him.*

12. Why do you think the author ends by describing Pip and Estella walking hand in hand—"as the morning mists had risen long ago when I first left the forge, so the evening mists were rising now"? What do you think will happen to Pip and Estella now? *Pip has high hopes for a happy life for Estella—just as he had high hopes when he left the forge to start his new life.*

Post-reading Discussion Questions

Literal Understanding

1. Who are these characters: Pip? Miss Havisham? Estella? Joe Gargery? Pumblechook? Orlick? Mr. Jaggers? Wemmick?
2. What is the connection between Pip, the convict, Miss Havisham, and Estella?
3. How does Pip "become a gentleman"?
4. How do Pip, Estella, and Miss Havisham change over the years?

Literary Analysis

1. Provide a time-line for the novel. Why do you think Dickens chose to have Pip tell the events of the story—in the order in which they happened, but years afterward? Could the story have been told better by an omniscient narrator? How does Pip change as he grows older? Do Miss Havisham and Estella change?
2. How does Dickens use movement in the novel, specifically movement between the marsh country where Pip lives as a boy, Miss Havisham's Satis House, and London?
3. How does imprisonment play a part in this novel—not just the convict's imprisonment, but also Miss Havisham's and other characters whose daily lives seem prisons?
4. How do the speech patterns of various characters—such as Joe, Pumblechook, and the convict—differ?
5. What coincidences occur in the novel? Does Dickens overdo coincidence in this story?
6. Find passages that show Dickens' use of sentimentality. For example, examine the scene where the convict dies with tears in his eyes. How do you feel about these instances of sentimentality?
7. How is history blended with fiction in this story?
8. Find passages where Dickens deliberately withholds information from his readers, but provides hints. Does this heighten interest in the story—or is it unfair and contrived?
9. Dickens loved theater. How is *Great Expectations* theatrical? To what moments does the novel build? Which scenes have "stagy" qualities?

Personal Interpretation

10. Which of the characters are most well-rounded? Which are the flattest? Which seem most real to you? Why?
11. This novel was written in installments. Why do you think "cliff hangers" are often found at the end of installments? What are some examples?
12. This has been called one of Dickens' "happiest" novels. Compare it to other novels by Dickens and explain why this one might be considered "happier." How does Dickens combine bitterness and laughter in *Great Expectations*?

Post-reading Extension Activities

Suggested Viewing
- Watch the 1946 movie version of *Great Expectations* and see what changes were made in the story when it was adapted for film. Critique the film, commenting on whether you think the changes improved or detracted from the novel's original story.

- Watch the five-hour-long 1988 BBC version of the novel. Compare it to the 1946 version—or write a review of the film with a partner. You should present opposite views. Enact the review in front of a video camera or in person for your class.

Writing
1. Rewrite the ending of the story so that Pip and Estella never get together. Compare your version with the one that Dickens originally intended (pp. 495-496). Which do you like best?

2. Choose one of the following themes and write an essay showing how it is developed in the course of the novel:
   - guilt
   - class divisions
   - the selfish pursuit of wealth
   - snobbery
   - moral rebirth
   - self-awareness

3. Write an essay in which you support or refute one of these statements, using evidence from the story:
   - In the end, Pip was what he wanted to be—a true gentleman.
   - In a class society, there is justice for the rich but none for the poor.
   - Class divisions sustained by wealth destroy the bonds of fellowship between men.

4. Compare and contrast Estella's real and adoptive mothers.

5. Write a character sketch of Wemmick. How is he like a modern-day commuter?

6. Explain the idea that this "is a violent book, and haunted, like the rest of Dickens' fiction, by jails and images of prison" (Introduction, p. 29) by tracing images of violence and prison throughout the book.

7. Go to your school or local library and find some criticism of *Great Expectations*. Read and react in writing to that criticism.

8. What themes does Dickens develop in this novel? Which of these themes are treated in other novels by Dickens? What insights does *Great Expectations* offer about the court system? about the independently wealthy? about the poor?

Language Study
1. Make a list of words and expressions found in the story, but no longer heard today (e.g., Dutch clock, jack-towel, give no one the office, etc.). Refer to the Notes at the end of the book for ideas.
2. Collect examples of figurative language (metaphors, similes, personification) found throughout the book.
3. Collect literary/biblical allusions made by Dickens throughout the book.

Art
1. Create a few simple props and stage a tableau depicting one of the more memorable scenes in the story (such as Pip and Estella playing cards while Miss Havisham watches, with the decaying wedding cake in the background).
2. Make a collage (magazine cut-outs and drawings pasted on cardboard) depicting a particular dream or memory sequence in the book (such as the nightmares young Pip has about the convict).
3. Make a stand-up character sketch of one of the characters by folding a piece of posterboard and drawing the character as you imagine him or her on one side. On the other side, describe the character using details from the story—as well as details that you imagine.

Music
1. Write Pip's story as song lyrics (to the tune of a well-known song).
2. Rewrite one chapter of the book as a radio play. Choose appropriate background music (that sets the proper mood and that Dickens might have known) and record the chapter on tape.

Drama
1. Write and act out a scene that appears in the story, such as the scene where Miss Havisham repents.
2. Write and act out a scene that is described, but not directly shown, in the story—such as the scene where Miss Havisham's will is read, or the scene where Jaggers defends Estella's mother in court.
3. Write and act out a scene that might occur if the story were extended or changed. For example, what are Pip and Estella doing 10 years after the close of the story? What might have happened if Pip, unaware of Joe's engagement, had told Joe that he planned to see if Biddy would have him?

Dance
1. Do a dance improvisation of a scene from the story, such as the scene where Pip crosses the marsh to bring the convict food and a file—or a scene where Pip's sister goes on the "rampage" with Tickler.

Research
1. Research several of the allusions in the book. For example, read the passage in St. Luke's gospel to which the second note in Chapter 56 refers: "The two men who went up into the Temple to pray..."
2. Find out more about the phrenologists to whom the convict refers in Chapter 42.
3. Research some of the patent medicines sold in Dickens' day (such as the Tar-water Pip's sister is fond of giving Pip).

Vocabulary List
Below is an extensive list of words found in *Great Expectations* which may need clarification and which you may wish to give to students. It is not our suggestion that students write definitions for so many words, but that they develop the habit of using a dictionary when they cannot determine an important meaning from context.

explicit 35	verification 47	intimated 57	liberal 63
nettles 35	decanted 47	hypothetical 57	joviality 64
lair 35	rimy 48	homily 57	fugitive 64
pollards 36	oppressed 48	prodigal 58	stipulated 64
vittles 37	cravat 48	gluttony 58	arid 64
file 38	obstinately 48	commiserating 58	dissociate 66
eluding 38	riveted 48	contumaciously 59	execrating 67
gibbet 39	despatch 49	misdemeanours 59	manacled 68
impregnable 40	ague 50	abhorrence 59	groveling 68
connubial 41	impelled 51	consternation 59	attentive 69
disconsolately 41	shrouded 52	expectorating 59	divergence 69
larceny 41	rank 52	omnipotent 60	drafted 70
avenging 41	chafe 52	imperiously 60	pilfering 71
foreshadowed 42	imprecations 52	terminated 60	exonerated 71
trenchant 42	prodigiously 53	genial 60	morbidly 72
apothecary 42	salutation 53	apparition 61	theological 73
plaister 42	conciliatory 53	coupling 62	catechism 73
safe 42	unceremoniously 53	bellows 63	liquidation 74
freemasonry 42	flounce 54	liberal 63	venerated 74
consternation 43	blithe 54	joviality 64	oracle 74
remonstrance 43	penitentials 54	fugitive 64	elaborated 75
aghast 43	dissuading 54	stipulated 64	purblind 75
bolting 43	banns 55	arid 64	cipher 75
elixir 44	vestry 55	dissociate 66	erudition 75
restorative 44	wheelwright 55	execrating 67	patronage 76
imbruing 44	chandler 55	manacled 68	meditative 77
constitutional 44	chaise-cart 55	groveling 68	judicial 77
garret 45	bobbish 56	attentive 69	perspicuity 77
augmented 45	juvenile 56	imperiously 60	sagaciously 78
emphatic 46	regaled 56	terminated 60	mogul 79
reproachful 46	goads 57	genial 60	replenish 80
interlocutor 46	declamation 57	apparition 61	sportive 81
deliverance 46	aspiration 57	coupling 62	barricaded 81
pall 47	presentiment 57	bellows 63	seclusion 81

Page numbers refer to the Penguin classics softcover edition.

Page numbers refer to the Penguin classics softcover edition.

Page numbers refer to the Penguin classics softcover edition.

Assessment for *Great Expectations*

Assessment is an ongoing process. The twelve Post-Reading Discussion Questions on page 29 of this guide as well as the Post-Reading Extension Activities on pages 30, 31, and 32, provide a wide variety of options. In addition writing exercises are included in the chapter-by-chapter section. Students will complete these activities during the novel study. Points may be tallied to indicate the level of understanding. As the activities are completed, both student and teacher check them off.

Name _____ Date _____

<u>Student</u>   <u>Teacher</u>

_____   _____   1. Write a review of one of the movie versions of *Great Expectations*, comparing it to the novel.

_____   _____   2. Rewrite the ending of the story so that Pip and Estella never get together.

_____   _____   3. Make a collage (magazine cut-outs and drawings pasted on posterboard) depicting a particular dream or memory in the book.

_____   _____   4. Make a list of words and expressions found in the story, but no longer heard today. Re-write the sentences using modern terms.

_____   _____   5. Write Pip's story as song lyrics (to the tune of a well-known song).

_____   _____   6. Act out a scene in the story with a partner.

_____   _____   7. Dramatize an alternate scene, then state why your scene is better than the one in Disckens' novel.

_____   _____   8. Collect and explain literary/biblical allusions made by Dickens throughout the book.

_____   _____   9. Research some of the patent medicines sold in Dickens' day, such as "tar-water."

_____   _____   10. Write a five-paragraph essay on one of the questions listed on page 29.

Notes

36